A CADENCE
OF DESPAIR

POEMS AND REFLECTIONS
ON HEARTBREAK, LOSS
AND RENEWAL

PRAISE FOR
A CADENCE OF DESPAIR

"In this brave and vulnerable book, Tenneson Woolf illustrates once again that we humans are made stronger at our broken and mended places. His mid-life descent, survival, and ascent into a man still in process is a profound map. We may try to avoid these dark corners, but whatever we, the reader, face will be strengthened by the light he shines."

> ~ **Christina Baldwin**, author of *Life's Companion*, *The Seven Whispers*, *Storycatcher*, and *The Circle Way*

"Tenneson has wandered the valleys of grief and the mountains of success. His poetry is a companioning prescription for anyone living life with all of its joys and sadnesses. These poems are soul-food – healthy and healing. Drink deep of these poems and be not alone."

> ~ **Charles LaFond**, author of *Note to Self: Creating Your Guide to a More Spiritual Life*

"In a piercing way, Tenneson touches the deeper heart strings and shadows that surround a center in us all. Look in this mirror to see what it means to rise above the darkness yet another time. What a common and necessary journey for each of us – and the whole family of humans at this time."

> ~ **Toke Moeller**, CEO Interchange, Cofounder of The Art of Hosting and The Flow Game

PRAISE FOR
A CADENCE OF DESPAIR

"Tenneson Woolf gives uncensored testament to the depth of pain that true surrender requires – important medicine for all of us who are willing to feel our own despair and the despair of the world."

~ **Kinde Nebeker** MFA, MATP-EP, Wilderness Rites of Passage Guide

"For those parched and bent from years of leaning into the winds of life, Tenneson's poems carry so much moisture. Come drink. Let them soothe, provoke, and grieve you. Let them hold you."

~ **Bob Stilger**, author of *After Now: When We Cannot See the Future, Where Do We Begin*

"Tenneson has captured raw material from dreams, journaling, places where the rational brain does not reign. This book is a radical act and generous gift!"

~ **Sarah MacDougall** Ed.D., Master Student and Elder of The Circle Way

"In his brave book, Tenneson embodies the courage of vulnerability and the grace of truth-telling. In his poetry and essays, Tenneson opens his heart to us, and invites us to open our hearts to life."

~ **Ann Pelo,** author most recently of *From Teaching to Thinking: A Pedagogy for Reiminaging Our Work*

PRAISE FOR
A CADENCE OF DESPAIR

"In Tenneson's willingness to share this deeply personal human journey, he touches the universal experience of coming face-to-face with, and questioning, the divine. I bow to his willingness to learn in public; we are all better for it."

~ **Quanita Roberson**, Grief Worker, West African Dagara Tradition

"I read these poems like I've read biblical Psalms. They are candid and honest. In this collection, Tenneson approaches the edge again and again, sometimes lingering frightfully. This is a book for people who look deeply into themselves."

~ **The Rev. Cameron Barr**, Senior Pastor, United Church of Chapel Hill

"Whenever anyone tells the truth about their experience, hiding nothing, we have the chance to recognize the human experience. Dark nights of the soul are an initiation into spiritual wisdom. Dwell with Tenneson in these poems and you'll know what this means. If you find yourself in these pages, you will have received the gift that Tenneson offers. "

~ **Margaret Wheatley,** author of many books including *Perseverance*, *Leadership and the New Science*, and *Who Do We Choose To Be*

A CADENCE OF DESPAIR

POEMS AND REFLECTIONS ON HEARTBREAK, LOSS AND RENEWAL

TENNESON WOOLF

CENTRESPOKE PUBLISHING
COMOX, BRITISH COLUMBIA

CENTRESPOKE PUBLISHING
Comox, BC   www.centrespoke.com

Canadian Cataloguing First Publication Date: March 2020

Woolf, Tenneson, 1962-

A CADENCE OF DESPAIR:
Poems and Reflections on Heartbreak, Loss and Renewal

ISBN 978-1-7751212-2-0 (softcover)

1. Poetry.   2. Renewal / Grief (Psychology).
3. Emotional Health.   I. Title.

Ordering Information
Special discounts are available on quantity purchases by bookstores, wholesalers, groups and individuals.

Cover design by germancreative (cover concept by CentreSpoke). Cover photo of author by Amanda Fenton.

FIRST EDITION
First Printing 2020

10 9 8 7 6 5 4 3 2 1

CONTENTS

*PERHAPS WE ALL HAVE A TEACHER OR TWO
THAT FEELS HARSH.
PERHAPS SOME OF THOSE TEACHERS,
THOUGH WE EVEN TRY TO AVOID THEM,
GUIDE US TO SOME OF OUR DEEPEST AND
MOST NEEDED INNER WORK.*

*I WANTED TO FEEL VITALITY
AND RICHNESS
WITHIN AND WITHOUT,
YET SO MUCH OF WHAT I KEPT FINDING
WAS DESPAIR.*

*I CAME TO KNOW DESPAIR
AS A COMPANIONING GUIDE,
EVEN A FRIEND,
BUT FOR A LONG TIME
IT SIMPLY WAS PUNISHING.*

DEDICATION

To Those Who Seek

To those whose circumstance
has taken them to the floor boards
of anguish and despair.

To those whose perseverance,
or even just luck,
has yielded an acceptance,
and even friendship,
with the floor boards.

To all those that seek
an honesty and discovery
from their inner worlds,
be that of despair, or joy,
or other awakenings,
that return us to our gifts.

ACKNOWLEDGEMENTS

THIS COLLECTION OF POEMS, STORIES, AND REFLECTIONS would not have happened without the friendship and skilled production direction of Roq Gareau. I want to thank him first for the soul brother that he is. He encouraged me with friendship to compile these poems to collection and to write with as much honesty as I could muster. Roq also carried this collection, bringing inspiration and renewal, when I was stuck and fearful. He took on an enormous task of sorting what to include and exclude, for which I am massively grateful.

I'm grateful for the group of Soultime men that, unbeknownst to me, were writing reflections for this book based on the poem sections shared with them. These are a group of men that meet twice per year, on an island off the west coast of Canada. It is in the yurt that we stir together deep remembering. Thank you to Bob, Lionel, Brian, Ross, Dave, Tom, Robert, John, Robi, and Roq. I love how the poems stirred deeply personal awakenings in them, and how they offered themselves through word and friendship, to lift me, each other, and the poems in this volume. Their reflections are attributed where included in the book. Everything else is me.

I'm grateful to Christina, who first taught me when I was participant in her writing workshop, "the first gift is that it heals us." I needed to remember that several times when I realized I was sharing very personal poems that allude to very personal material. Christina helped me to see more of the bridge between what is personal and what is universal. She also offered crisp and incisive eye to drafts of this collection.

I'm grateful to Meg, who has encouraged me over twenty years to "let the words write you." She has been a stalwart friend and guide that has laughed with me and offered wisdom that helped me further surrender to being written.

I'm grateful to so many other friends that encouraged authenticity and honesty, even when all of that was, and is, still rather messy – that's what the broader emotional landscapes are supposed to be. It was cups of tea or coffee. It was reading and commenting. It was listening ears and hearts.

I'm grateful to family. My parents, Myrna and Dave, and my deceased father, Gary. My parents always encouraged me to remain true to myself and provided emotional bedrock for me to figure out a bit more of the sticky parts of what that means.

I'm grateful to my sister, Wendy, together with whom I hold an undying connection, even across miles. To my grandmothers and grandfathers who so often lifted me when I had no idea I needed to be lifted – I often feel them near, though each has passed from this life. To my aunts, uncles, and cousins that formed me as young boy and young adult, and helped me by just being the good and steady people that they are.

I'm grateful to my kids and their partners – oh how magical it has been to be with them as a dad, and to be unforgettably marked by their hearts and spirits.

With appreciations that go so much beyond words.

WELCOME

WITHIN A DARK WOODS

"In the middle of the journey of our life I found myself within a dark woods where the straight way was lost."
~ Dante Alighieri, Inferno, 14th Century Italian Poet

THERE ARE MANY OF US THAT FACE OUR DARK WOODS, losing the straight way. The journey into the dark woods impacts those that journey and those that wait for us at the forest edge. This journey happens with unique nuance for men, enculturated so often to not speak of such hell. I choose to speak of the dark woods.

These poems, stories, and reflections are not intended as happy. Consider yourself warned. If you need happy, stop now. Find something else.

These are honest expressions. Written from as much clarity as I could find, and with an awareness learned from one of my writing teachers – "the first gift is that it heals us."

These poems come from night-time dreams with many characters, from waking-life experience, from personal journey – sometimes written as I experienced them, and sometimes morphed by me to more universal experience.

2018 was a very difficult year for me. I was struggling significantly to find any healing and meaning.

I was in what would come to be, the end of a marriage. I'd thought that what was ahead was reconciliation and stripes earned to stand together in well-earned trouble.

I guessed wrong and unfairly.

Initially, I thought these writings might be more exclusively for men. Men in loss and grief and despair, who might benefit from a bit of permission to be in loss and grief and despair. But I think these writings may be for women too. We are all trying to show up with each other.

2018 was a year in which I felt most challenged. Most suicidal. Most in despair. Most panicked. Most lost. It was as if within my kitchen cupboards, each of these – challenge, suicidal wonder, despair, panic, and loss – were items that I just wanted to discard, to be rid of. And sometimes I thought I had, only to return the next day to find the same cans reproduced in my cupboards.

My dark woods was the end of marriage, yes. But it was, even more so, stuff before that coming to a kind of very difficult culmination. So many days and nights were despair filled.

I sought solace in writing, mostly in my private journal. Sometimes blurting things in splotches of 3-4 pages. Sometimes unfolding a bit of essence in a mere 3-4 lines.

I didn't seek to be neat and tidy.

In 2019, it occurred to me that if I were transparent with my despair written in my journal, it might not just help with my wellness, but also might help others with theirs too. I sought meaning from my journey and an arc of healing.

These poems and stories come from that journal. Morphed messages and dreams transcribed. Dark nights keyboarded into bits of prose, and steps of cadence.

Let me stretch it one more layer – these are, in a way, love poems. To self. To other. To an idea. To a loss. To dare to speak them into being is to show a kind of love.

People have often told me I'm thoughtful, and that I'm articulate. I'm grateful for that. I'm mostly wanting to speak authentically, with just enough sweeping to attend to the mess, and yet grown ability to walk on floors where broken shards and debris remain. Perhaps to welcome this authenticity in others too.

Read on if you seek this. There is a progression that emerged for me that you will see in the chapter titles, from raw and dark to beginning glimpses of sunlight, to rebounds into more darkness, and to new path and integration. Read quickly if you must. Or slowly, a couple of pieces at a time. Or just one section, with pause. Follow what calls you. And follow where your inner poetry leads you.

I hope that you find within you, your own cadence and authenticity, and even friendship, with despair. For me, I had to.

FOREWORD

LINES OF GOLD
R o q   G a r e a u

IF THE MAP OF A PERSON IS A STORY, Tenneson is one of the most courageous cartographers that I know. In this daring assortment of poems, he uses words like a torch to expose hidden-in-the-corner truths and cast shadows beyond the load-bearing fictions that underlie the blueprint of his life. It is only the individual who has left their established territory and toured strange lands that can build a bridge to expand the small world and insufficient identity they once occupied.

Guided into these poems, Tenneson passes through a very dark place. In that darkness, he sacrifices the debased currencies of naivety, comfort, and habit, to find a golden thread that, when followed, provides the dignity to stand up from the floorboards and re-enter the world.

Like Tenneson in his underworld struggle, we are all different amalgams of limitation and potential, seeking to forge a new coherence out of tradition, necessity, heartbreak, and change. On descending journeys, it is essential to update outdated operating systems, and hopefully, with some help along the way. At such pivotal times, a circle of trusted people that provides the space for major reformation and editing can be immensely valuable. Humans do a better job together – particularly in groups built of reciprocity, personal responsibility, and truth-telling. I continue to learn this from Tenneson – in how he carries, expresses and shares himself and these poems, and also in how he has approached this writing project as a whole.

This book of poems was assisted by a small band of men who gather in retreat twice a year to explore the initiatory moments in life that shear meaning and eclipse purpose from individual narratives. The challenge to write, and the support to face the tremendous inner-conflict, insecurity, anxiety, and depression therein, emerged within this shelter of belonging. I am a better person for having shared that space with these men; particularly by bearing witness to and collaborating with Tenneson on this volume of healing.

The core learning forged by my friendship with Tenneson goes something like, "If you want to get closer to someone, share a fault – and while you're there, try to fill it with gold."

It is risky business to forsake familiar stances and become strange sons and daughters of chaos. The world reveals itself through the incomplete, flawed, beautiful story of the individual. And the human story of transformation – of leaving home and returning with some cracks filled with gold – is very much a contradiction to despair.

INTRODUCTION

BEFRIENDING DESPAIR

IT'S EARLY MORNING. By that, I mean middle of the night, often between 2:00 and 3:30 a.m. I wake, and then lay awake, just as I do for many middles of the nights. Sometimes, I wake in my bed. Sometimes, on the floor, where I'd collapsed myself into sleep the night before, craving the lowest elevation I could find. Sometimes, in the closet where I'd try to cocoon my fears and despair. I wake hoping that it isn't time to get up. Because I'm afraid that I can't muster the energy to face another day. I want to remain longer, in oblivion, removed from the waking world and the despair that has come to grip me.

Eventually, of course, middle of the night would give way to start-the-day morning, often 5:30 or 6:00 for me. I've been an early riser most of my life. However in these despair-gripped days, often, I'd remain in bed, or on the floor, or in the closet until 7:30, 8:30, or 9:30 unable to will myself to morning routine. On those days, I would often fill good parts of the morning in prayer. By prayer, I mean begging. Begging God, gods, ancestors, family both living and passed, "Please, please, please – help me make it through this day. Please, please, please – help me make it through this day."

I was so afraid. Afraid that my worries and fears, my unresolved and, at that point, completely hijacking worries, would tip me and my inner imposter into unrecoverability. That I would completely lose any last worn thread that connected me to competency. Or respectability. Or lovability. I feared that I would completely lose all of it.

I feared being embarrassed. I feared being exposed, or revealed, as the mess that I was. "Please, please, please." Sometimes I begged from head under covers. Sometimes I begged from laying on my back, staring at blank ceiling. Sometimes I begged from obsessive pacing back and forth in hallway, as if I might walk away my challenges.

This begging was most intense over a three year period, in my fifties. But it feels like other more subtle versions had been with me much of my life, mostly masked to me and to the outer world (I hoped).

I've learned that all of that, those deep fears, ironically, can live among great joys, which I suppose is what builds fear in many of us – that honesty with despair will negate or remove our joys. My great joys include family, children, professional success, love, friendship. It's odd, isn't it? Many of us expend lots of effort to negate our fears and despairs, rationalizing them away as momentary departures from the joy. Yet these all go together, in a kind of cadence.

In these pages, I offer much of what I've learned, daring to befriend despair. I didn't seek this kind of writing. It just became, eventually, unavoidable. I've wondered, often, if this friendship would have been better left undeveloped or ignored.

By befriend, I don't mean immediate and joyful infatuation. Befriending despair has been more slow, confusing, and requiring patience with failing and trying again, and sometimes just giving up.

What I've learned has very much been that it is significant and important to develop a relationship with these most seemingly personal, yet in the end, universal human experiences – despair, grief, loss, wonder, hope, love.

We don't "do" despair or "do" love so that we can then be done with them. We come to know them like we know our feet or hands. We come to know capabilities and limits with both gratitudes and a few laments.

I write these words with hope that they might help create access and relationship for others with their versions of despair, and, thus with more awakened honesty of being human and in human communities. It's a bit of permission to claim what we deny…

CHAPTER 1

PAIN, GRIEF AND SHAME

I T IS 2008. I'M ROLLING ON THE FLOOR of my newly rented, furniture-less, townhome living room. By rolling, I mean agonizing. Crying out. I'm in deep emotional pain. Yes, it is shame. And grief. And loss. I am separated from my wife. I am separated from my children. I don't know it yet, but I'm separated from myself. This townhome is deliberately close to where my kids remain living. I'm doing anything I can to soothe or numb the pain. And grief. I don't know it yet, but these are old and unresolved pains from much earlier in life, amplified by separation. I don't know it yet, but I'm about to enter a high fever of personal emotional work. I'm about to re-sort everything that is in the kitchen cupboards of my inner world. I'm about to begin to journey through ten years of transformation (and there's no way that I can call it that at this point) with what I've most often denied, run from, or buried in my emotional landscape.

Fast forward a few years of that transformation in which I've developed more relationship with pain, grief, and shame. I'm no longer in high fever. It is August 2011. I've flown from my home in Utah to Fairbanks, Alaska. I'm meeting my friend Roq who I've now known for five years. He's been temporarily stationed in the north for work and will be returning by car to his home near Vancouver, British Columbia. He's invited me to drive with him. It's 2,500 miles. We will do this over five days.

I'm excited about this trip. Roq is a good friend. He's smart. Kind. Thoughtful. He loves to create and explore ideas together. He has unique way of moving fluidly between the profound and the silly. I love that in a friend. I also love the thought of five days in the container that is car. It's mostly talking with each other, flowing from serious to silly to serious. We are asking questions of each other, each taking time to respond. We are sharing stories with each other. In the road trip that is return.

I ask Roq, as we are shifting topics, driving through the wild of the north and the wild of our inner landscapes, "Anything you feel shame for?" The question arose spontaneously from me. It wasn't calculated. Roq and I trust each other. And we trust what the road trip opens for us. "Ah, now that's a good question," Roq shares. He's licking his chops. He knows that this is a unique invitation for two men to share.

We proceeded to share not-told stories. We proceeded to release moments of shame, as Roq would later come to name as "draining the pond of shame." Shame from childhood. From current life. From family. From profession. We proceeded to celebrate the sharing of inner worlds. With no judgement. In fact, the opposite, with celebration of shames – "that's a good one." Only witnessing, so that judgement could be released. Or reoriented. I didn't know it then, but came to learn that there is healing in the telling, and in the realization that shame, like love and joy, is also universal.

Pain, grief, and shame (maybe guilt too) – these are close familial cousins from the inner, often hidden emotional world. They overlap. Yet, they are nuanced. So many of us have unknowingly bought into fears of our images being tarnished through honest reveals of shame, grief, and guilt. I have learned much later in life than I want to admit (there's the shame again), how significant it is to come into relationship with these three cousins, or as psychotherapist and grief worker Francis Weller shares of grief, "to come into an apprenticeship."

It was that day with Roq, in the company of just he and me, with passing open vistas of Yukon and northern British Columbia, yet the bounded container of two men in the front seats of a car – that I felt cracked open to a transformation in relationship with grief, shame, and guilt – from rejection and embarrassment to more welcome and integration.

In the coming eight years I would toggle significantly with these three cousins. Accepting. Rejecting. Accepting. Rejecting. Yes, I was apprenticing with them. I was learning new frameworks. I was also, at times, reeling on the floor, agonizing at losses. I didn't want to hurt. I didn't want to hurt others or let them down. I was very afraid, in this confrontation with what was both outer, but also, inner reality. I didn't want to crumble – this crumbling is one of the lies that contemporary society tells us about witnessing and acknowledging pain, and grief, and shame. The fire of these cousins was at times too much for me to bear. There were many moments when I felt I simply would not make it. I would just be consumed with loss of family, of spouse, of colleagues, of country – and again, loss of self, that turned out to be required, so as to find self.

These poems are about some of all that, they are about daring to travel with the untraveled.

Sipping Soda

"How are you?" he asked,
in the coffee shop, The Commons.
We each sipped a sparkling soda,
black cherry, in the late afternoon,
on which yellow daffodils swayed outside
in light wind and rain.

I searched for words
that would be honest,
not wanting to miss
that moment of old friendship,
that had us face to face
swaying together.

"I'm dangerously lonely,"
I said.

Then we sipped more soda,
and followed the lonely together.

On the Floor

I slept in the closet,
and on the floor, again,
unchanged from my day clothes.

Confinement,
please comfort me.

Help me to face this aloneness,
help me to change.

I wish worry could be over,
worry that makes me unavailable
for the fulfilled want.

Off Center, Fucking Rattled

I get off center
(by that I mean fucking rattled)
when I do not trust
in the stories I share,
in the experience that I know,
and in the teachings that I create.

I get fucking rattled,
thinking that I need to be
something other than what I am,
that I must once again,
abandon myself
to have belonging.

That's fucked.

Touched High and Centered

"You can put people to sleep,"
he told me.

"Push on this nerve-ending
that is high and centered
on the back."

"Then catch the person," he said,
"to gently put them on the floor."

I wonder, sometimes,
if I am asleep,
touched high and center.

Wake

I wake.
Yet I want to sleep.
I don't want the day to strip me of infinity.

I feel.
Yet I want to numb.
I don't want the pain to debilitate anymore.

Why is this depression so hard?

Something or someone
whispers to me,
love yourself first.

Exhausting

It is exhausting
to feel
that I'm never off,
that I always
need to be thinking
about what is next
or about how
I must advantage myself.
Exhausting.

People Get Hurt

Fear is palpable in this dream,
as people sit in rows of black, wooden chairs.

Uncertainty is thick,
with life itself about to be unseated.

Danger is moot,
well past a mere possibility.

People get hurt,
and I wish it wasn't so.

I don't want
to sit in this chair.

Unanchored

It was two years ago today
that she died.

I had come to see her
in her passing.

She was one of my anchors.
I feel a bit unanchored these days.

This Funeral

I want to be on time to this funeral.
There is death, loss of someone I love.
There is also death in me.

Yet, we arrive late.
The burial has already taken place,
far away in the valley.

It was then,
in my anger and grief
that I lost it,
and wept uncontrollably,
into her shoulder
over all of it.

Rough Patch

I can't stand myself.
Declining further and further.
Disappointing people around me.
Not being honest.
Wishing life would deliver me,
or deliver something to me.
Hating life, for the way it withholds.
Feeling immature about all of that.
This is a rough, rough, rough patch.

Withheld

It might also be true
that I withhold happiness –
I deny it –
to protect me
from too much
disappointment and loss.

Aching in Transition

Yesterday I wanted to die.
The pain was too much.
The pain of feeling as though
I've failed my kids.

Just like I learned was true
for my Dad.
But much later, after he'd taken his own life –
he hadn't failed me.

Doing Here?

What
in the world
am I
doing here?

Last Night

Last night I begged for ancestors
to come to me.
I can't stand living on the mere possibility
of another world.
I need something real.
Real enough.
What the fuck do you want from me?
Why the fuck do you torment me?
I'm close to losing it.

Small Glasses of Beer

It was him
and his dog
and me.

We were drinking
small glasses of beer.

I meant to be playful
plopping my emptied glass
in front of him.

But it hairline cracked.

We laughed.
But I still felt bad.

I've made mistakes
in this life.

Created hairline cracks
and mass shattered shards.

But I really could use
some laughter now.

Like with a friend and his dog
and small glasses of beer.

Way Too Much Food

Sometimes,
I eat
way too much food.

I know
that I'm trying
to consume matter
to fill an aching vacancy.

There is a scarcity
that can never be filled
by more consumption.

Steal the Show

I have learned
that shame
and failure
always seem ready,
to not only make
an appearance,
but to
steal the show.

Inescapable Grief and Shame

In this place of respite
that only a brothering friend could offer,
in simple home,
near top of world,

I've ambled along high mountain road,
with no particular place to go.
I've hiked unbounded back country,
eyes open for bears.
I've watched a downloaded TV program,
wishing transport away from myself,
from my thinking,
from deeper heart pain.

I've tried to finish
writing
about "wander"
and about "life energy."

I've despised what I've written.

I've held ceremony,
stones shaken and placed in four directions,
and other items left behind
forever to be on this mountain,
like I wish I could be left behind.

I've slept,
like cat in afternoon sun,
hours on
mountain facing deck.

I've skipped food,
wishing release.
I've gorged on food,
also wishing release.

I've paced the floors,
as one does when on the edge of kooky.

I've strummed guitar,
aching for sound to deliver
something from me.

I've stared out the window.
into inescapable grief and shame.

Never, Ever, Again

Never, ever, again –
do I want to abandon myself
in such denial,
or manipulation,
of what is inherently
true.

In Trouble

I am in trouble.

I am closing down.
Not wanting to be with anyone.
I am shaking with fear.
My shoulders are very tight.
I feel like I'm going to puke.

PAIN, GRIEF AND SHAME
Reflection by Bob Timms:

I HAVE LEARNED THROUGH MY 70 YEARS that I should be thankful for having experienced all my impressionable life events. After years of soul work, the kind that Tenneson's poems point to, I can now pick-up each experience one at a time and remember the suffering in them that has gradually formed my character of today.

It's not that I am less fearful. By clumsily confronting my own trouble, with a lot of help from my friends, I have become more brave and more integrated.

Hard stories, like those shared by Tenneson, remind me that courage is earned, particularly when learning the hard way. It's hard-earned courage, witnessed by others, that lifts the weight of heavy memories off of our shoulders, so that we may continue on the journey.

CHAPTER 2

LOSS

I AM SITTING IN THE EARLY MORNING DARK OF MY ROOM. On my bed. My back is leaned against wall. I'm staring into textured shadow and shape of a corner palm plant, grown now floor to ceiling, impressively. I like that this plant is, well, alive. I like that it holds itself persistently and unashamedly, even in the dark of my room, perhaps trusting that afternoon sun will arrive, at which point it will instinctively twist to touch warmth and light. I have blanket wrapped around me to keep me warm. Perhaps also to help me feel contained. I want to feel held. I want to feel that I'm OK. I want to be like my palm plant, still able to touch.

On this particular morning, loss feels, comparatively, more. Loss has a way of growing the most human of emotions – unease, insecurity, failure – from "tiny bit irritation" to "heaping bunch intensity." "Oh dear," I think to myself, trying to wrap into more comfort. I feel huge personal and professional responsibilities coming to light in my day, and the urgencies that go with them, and what has become regular fear that I won't be able to fulfill them.

On this particular morning, "imposter syndrome me" is boisterous. A bunch. And lots of self-criticism.

Because, here it comes again, "people who have it 'together' don't experience loss" – yah, that's a punishing storyline for many of us. A stupid one too. Nonetheless, I can feel myself trying way too hard, wrestling against the choke-holds of loss. I can feel myself over-compensating. I keep "trying so hard" because that's one of the walls that I lean back to, that I love from my family system. We "work hard." Yet I know that this efforting isn't going to get me home – I'll need something different.

I'm searching frantically in my psyche for what's missing and why loss feels so strong today. I search through immediate circumstance of loss. But I know this movie has played much further back to my childhood. I thought I'd done enough inner work to never feel this way again. To never feel this kind of loss again. To never feel this kind of wound again. I thought it was gone from the room. It turns out it was just over in that dark corner.

We all experience loss. If you are human, it's not "is there loss?" Rather, it's "are you willing to look for it, sometimes in the dark, when all you have is a wall to lean against?" Loss of a friend. Or a dog. Maybe a thing. Maybe a memory. Maybe the path in the forest that is life purpose. Loss that reveals impermanence in what we thought was permanence. "Oh, how many times must I circle around on loss? How many times must I surrender?"

As I sit in my room, on the bed, wrapped in blanket, wishing to be protected, wishing to be protected more, I start to hear morning crows outside my window, up in the trees, doing their caws. No matter how much I face my losses, or run from them, or deny, or avoid, or turn to, the crows continue their caws. Something in that makes me feel happy.

Learning to accept loss, this most human of experience that so often dances with despair, is what these coming poems point to for me. They point both into and through the wound. Both into and through the hurt and anger. Both into and through the blame that we sometimes heap upon ourselves and others.

Until We Weren't

We were friends
for a long while.

Laughing.
Loving.
Playing.
Growing.
Wondering.
Dreaming.

Until,
We weren't

Reclaiming Competence

I would like
to reclaim
a competence
that I lost
somewhere.

It turns out
I do not need
to abandon
myself.

Not to belong,
nor to feel loved,
nor to have security,
nor to have clarity.

Done

Done

I can feel now,
more clearly,
that our paths
forward
are not together.

No Railing

This high balcony,
it has no railing.

Safety here is an illusion,
marked only by another edge,
and free fall.

Caution no longer protects,
and there is nowhere to hide
in this unbounded grief.

There is no return to comfort.

Failed Flight

Despite enough apparent speed
and continued attempts at correction
we never got off the ground.

Instead
there was great damage,
even wreckage.

Now
I just want to
walk home.

He Is So Far Away Now

I am learning
again

that inner work
is a practice.

Doubt's persistence
reaffirms

that going alone
is so tiring.

He is so far away,
now.

Not My House

I'm now in your house.
I'm not intruder, but rather, helping you
with what invades.

I don't know your rooms.
I'm just seeking to protect you, quietly.

Soul Work

This is soul work.
Trouble.

Trouble from which
one is gifted more trouble.

I don't think many of us know

that this hurting and denying,
we do with each other,

this is trouble,
that is the soul work.

I'm OK with That

Travel to far away places,
this we did.

Create rituals and intimacy,
this too we did.

Miss you,
I will.

But I'm OK with that.

Gained My Freedom

You are wounded,
like the ones you came from,
they said.

I gained my freedom
when I realized,
that was only kind of true.

A Certain Joy

Time to rest.
These days have been intense.

Getting clear always is.
So is letting go.

And then, I'm glad,
these are followed with a certain joy.

Isn't About This

Failure in this,
isn't about this.

Nor is the rage,
or the shame,
or the hurt,
or the fear.

It's often about that,
long ago,
that wasn't even mine.

The Memories You Ask For

I've done my best
to sort through the months and years.

I just don't have them,
the memories you ask for.

I just can't find them.
I'll need to leave those with you,
unresolved.

LOSS

Reflection by Lionel Philippe:

A SINGLE CHOICE HAS a ripple effect, big and small. My six-year-old daughter had asked me to stay, but I didn't. Sometimes, I wonder what might have happened if I would have stayed. Of course, I will never know.

Looking back, I can see how self-centered I was, and how closed my heart was to the pain and loss I had caused others.

I have not seen my daughter in nine years. Now, at the age of 24, and a parent herself, she has a four-year-old son, whom I have never met. Sometimes I create stories of an imagined future that only yield to me more pain and sorrow.

I miss my daughter. I would like to know who she is now, what she likes and doesn't like, what challenges she has faced and where she has succeeded. I'd love to hear her perspective on motherhood, relationship and family.

When I became a parent at 36, I had no clue how to be a father. Honestly, I still don't. The truth is, I don't know my daughter. I don't know my grandson. These are losses that I grieve.

Tenneson knows about loss. Even though his losses are different than mine, he helps by writing about what is more common and universal. There is loss that I need to face, express and repair before I die. It feels appropriate to say that out loud – to write it down. What remains unsaid, remains irreparable.

If I fail to see my daughter again, or never meet my grandson, I want to feel the inner assurance that I have done the best that I can to find my way back into her heart, and to the generations that follow.

Loss teaches me.

CHAPTER 3

HINTS AND INSIGHTS

I REMEMBER DECEMBER in Edmonton, Alberta. I am 12-13 years old. Christmas is nearing. There is snow on the ground. One of my responsibilities is to shovel the sidewalks. I do that. I'm proud of it. I also do a little of the neighbors' sidewalks because it is neighborly. I'm also seeking approval through pleasing. Some from my single mom. Some from my neighbors. I didn't know it explicitly then, but I was a kid that, in addition to being rather playful, sporty, and good at math, also worried. I didn't know it then, but I was a kid that, in addition to feeling very appreciated, supported, and that did pretty well in school, also feared a kind of "not OK" and "not belonging."

As Christmas nears, I'm awaiting my Grandparents arriving. These are Mom's parents, Fern and Billie. They were, to me, the heart of Christmas from those younger years. When they arrive after their four-hour drive from Saskatchewan, that means to me that Christmas is really on. I love them. We all do. My aunts and uncles. My cousins. We are a family that spends a lot of time together. Drinking cups of tea. Eating cookies that Grandma has made. Playing ping pong and card games. The world seems OK when Granny and Gramps arrive.

I didn't know it then, but Christmas was one of two times when I felt a tangible layer of my inner, young-boy-worry, subside, replaced in me, with a kind of glee. I didn't know it then, but that glee was palpable belonging. It was palpable "I'm OK" and palpable "held by family."

One of the hints from this recalled Christmas family memory of 45 years ago is that, no matter how much I might believe or convince myself that I've got all the unknowns and uncertainties of my life figured out, there's plenty of unresolved stuff too. It gets stuffed down. And eventually lays dormant, but not disappeared.

In my added wisdom of 45 years, I've come to realize that all people have unresolved experience and story. All of us have experience of loss, or "not OK," or "not belonging." So the hint that accompanies that kind of despair material is that there is much more to become aware of, that can render us more able to meet people in their versions of unresolvedness.

Shift the context. I remember it as summer a few years later. I am camping in central Alberta. I'm 15 or 16 now. I'm going to walk along the river, on my own, into the unpeopled forest. I need this. I'm not sure why. There are bears here. Cougar too. Deer. I need to be a bit careful. "Just stay close to the river," I remind myself. I'm walking, hiking, and tramping in areas that are quite remote. The best I can find is animal trails. The best I can find is myself. And I love this. I go for a couple of hours. It's not the smartest thing – shouldn't do it alone – but I'm compelled by the home that I feel in the forest. I cross the river a few times. I climb steep banks. I slide on slippery stones. I'm OK here. It's palpable, just like when Granny and Gramps arrive for Christmas. I belong here. I don't worry about things here. The forest companions me.

I've had to learn, through numerous hints, that wounds can feed and develop strengths. Mine. Yours. Ours. That's not a marketing pitch to bypass the pain of wounds. I've had to learn that all humans experience wound. Most of us eventually find our way to the dark woods. Contemporary society tries to obliterate that narrative. Or shame it. Or oversimplify it, stripping us of the inherent wholeness that our wounds certify. It is my experience that contemporary society so often compounds avoidance with its own cumulative and unaddressed collective grief. I've had to learn to treat self and other with kindness around such things.

I've had to learn, through hints, that our wounds don't require a resolved relationship where everything is all better. It's not a comfort bandage that our wounds ask of us. It's not tossing the cans from the cupboard – it's knowing what lives there, and perhaps being able to selectively lock or unlock the cupboard. Our wounds ask for us to let them gift us with the learning and maturing that only come with wound, struggle, descent, and sometimes scar. They often can show the way to initiatory path, in which we find ourselves more able to understand and help with the complexity of the times in which we live.

These poems bring some of that hint energy, some a-ha and insight that uniquely comes from despair's offering of renewal.

I'm More Skilled Now

I've been hurt
in the directions I chose.

I'm more skilled now.
From practice.
From insight.
From courage.

I'll likely
still get hurt again.

But perhaps,
more skilled again, too.

Alone, Except When I'm Not

It is another day
waking up
in my home
by myself.

There is nobody.
Not my dog
Not my kids.
Just me.

It takes effort
for me to lift my legs
out of my bed
again.

Perhaps by grace alone,
it occurs to me

that maybe
this is opportunity
to welcome

and watch
for the invisible beings,
and the less visible beings,
that accompany me.

It occurs to me
that I am alone,
except when I'm not,
which is maybe, always.

Penetrated Psyche

Not enough.
Not competent.
Imposter.
Unlovable.

These thoughts
penetrate
one's psyche

Beware of Fusion

Last night
I dreamt
that together,
we were
helping a young,
late-twenties couple,
reconcile
their relationship.

Last night
in the dream
I told them
to be
careful
with fusion
and then,
I woke.

What to Remember

What to remember,
when meeting a former partner,
when neither moving together,
nor moving apart.

Perhaps nothing.
Just being in the moment.

I Suppose

I suppose that my hope is that
this inner journey is refining me.

I suppose that my hope is that
I am daring to lean in to the wound and anger
of leaving innocence and ignorance.

I suppose that my hope is that
I will find integration and wisdom.

I suppose that my hope is that
I am connected to divinity,
either approved by God, or in sync enough.

I suppose that my hope is that
I am loved and accepted.

I'm becoming aware that this only happens
in the external
when it is happening
in the internal.

This Battle

I can see this battle
from my bunker house.
I suppose I'm safe.

I can see that this battle
is old.

It started before me.

Similarities and Differences

I like our similarities.
I also like our differences.

It's Good to Return

It's good to return
I'm glad to have my son pick me up
at the airport.
I love seeing full-leafed rhubarb in my garden,
and flowering petunias,
and zucchini beginning to grow.

It's good to return
to neighbors that have sorted yard care,
as children laugh in playground.

It's good to return
to salad as a meal,
and regular exercise,
and watching "our show"
with my boy.

There is power in return,
There is comfort in return.
Just as there is in the journey.

I Can Read These Symbols

It was a large cave,
very red in color,
with hieroglyphs all over the walls.

I can read these symbols.
I don't know exactly why.

I can distinguish subtlety of different forms
grouped in lines and triangles.

I am a translator.
I always have been.
I don't know exactly why.

Keeps Me Going

The unseen,
spirit,
and life's inherent flow,
have always,
compelled me.

I tried church.
And it tried me.

But it is my dreams,
and a somewhat aware
gut feeling,
that keep me going.

Enough

When I was baptized
into that church
thirty-six years ago,
I so wanted belonging.

I wanted to feel spirit.
I wanted it to find me.

Today,
I just slow my pace,
I drink tea,
I feel for my mind and for my heart.

And it feels like enough.
Sometimes, even, that I am enough.

Odd

It's odd, right.

To feel left out
of a story
that we don't even
really want,
but nonetheless,
hurt
over being left out of.

Doesn't Require

I hope
that this friendship
doesn't require
me
to abandon myself.

Be Kind

The offer to help
is kind.

It expresses connection
and ability.

The receiving of help
is also kind.

It too,
grows connection,
and just helps.

Be kind.

Abrupt Difference

I don't like
at all
the abrupt difference
I know

that is between
the freedom of
life unfolding,
with its inherent expansion,

and of life contracting,
with its rigid obligation
and collapse.

That Advice

That advice that I can so easily find for someone
that I love,
that heartfelt imploring,
or that animated impatience,
is that advice that I so obviously need for myself.

I'm Descending

I'm descending now
to more of the unseen,
the mysterious,
and perhaps,
mythical world,
that abides deep below
mountain surface.

I've asked for this journey
from the gods.

Pleaded really.

Things feel a bit distorted to me
in this descent,
in this surrender,
that scratches and scrapes
at my psyche,
yet transforms everything.

I don't want to resist.

Grows Between Us

Commitment
will always
matter.

I hope that
that
grows between us

in the most
matured
of ways.

Light Orange and Silver

I think God
might just be
among
the murmuring
school of fish,
light orange
and silver.

Invoked

Tumble forward
with life,
or whatever you feel as divine.

Plan when needed,
with the best of brain, heart, and belly,
or whatever you feel is gut true.

Let go, often.
The elders have always
invoked this deeper trust.

Nutso

Some people are just
plain crazy.

Nutso with fabricated story
and corroborated weak evidence.

I feel deeply saddened
to say this.

For I suppose
this is true of me too.

To See

In my night dream
a person fired a bullet
through my eye.

I could see it coming,
slow motion.
It was vivid and disturbing.

In this waking day life
I have this feeling that it takes the eyes
that are behind eyes
to see.

HINTS AND INSIGHTS
Reflection by Brian Hoover:

W HEN POETS ENTER into the territory of hints and insights, the world of the periphery opens up. What is implied and not entirely clear becomes the often elusive expression of the world we live in. That is, the world of black and white fades into a misty gray and the definite is called into question.

Whenever something is hinted at, it often means that the subject material may be too sensitive to approach head-on. There are lots of cases where direct confrontation is a foolish strategy. Hinting at something is also an invitation to the recipient to engage in a solution, perhaps invoking a creativity that is collaborative. Now that's gold! This becomes very valuable in a time when there is so much one-way, top-down expression bombarding us. These poems draw us into a collaborative space. The practice of "reading between the lines" is activated and the ability to discern what is really being expressed is called upon.

Another aspect of the hint is how it awakens the riddle. The psyche loves a good riddle. The act of puzzling is an ancient one and addresses the deepest questions like who are we, where do we come from and where are we going? Poets freely leave us wondering and from the state of wonder the misty world beyond right and wrong gives way to difference without judgement.

The realm of insight is, of course, the territory of the seer. Literally, in-sight takes us into the psyche. Poetry flourishes here partly because the image takes precedent over the explicit meaning of the words. Just as the map is not the territory, the words of a poem are not so much explanatory as evocative. In such a way then, the poet is a translator and one that doesn't necessarily know why they are moved to write their poetry. They are allowing a deeper meaning to flow through them. Surrender is often the only way to be guided in these depths. The intuition and "gut-feelings" are methods of transport in these worlds where there is fortitude to be found. Poets are thereby allowed to go to dangerous and dark places that in the everyday world may be considered crazy.

"What is madness but the nobility of the soul at odds with circumstance," says the poet Theodore Roethke.

May we all take a moment every day, stop what we are doing, take down a book of poetry, bless the poets and reflect on the great wisdom granted us by their courageous journeys.

CHAPTER 4

INTIMACY AND FRIENDSHIPS

IT IS SUMMER. I am following up via video phone with a friend and colleague Moze, who I've known for a few years, but only met in person once, a year prior. We've made email reference to one another about the awe and beauty in our respective lives. I love Moze's energy. I love the way she speaks. I love how she frames her life and her work with such honesty and vulnerability. I love the friendship we are growing. It has the feeling of just right timing.

On one of our calls, Moze shares some of her doubts about a person that she has come to know. It is a doubt in trust and honest communication – it's also a doubt, which many of us have, underneath that of worthiness for genuine affection. Moze then contrasts her perception of people in honesty and affection with me. "Oh, everybody loves Tenneson," she tells me.

Wait, what?

I like the sound of what she was saying, but found it difficult to believe. She must mean "like." She must mean "some people." In despair, I'd lost some simple awareness and clarity. In my brain, and heart, and overall being, it was the opposite of what she was saying. It was that nobody loved me, nor liked me, nor counted me as creative. None of it. The tank was empty for me. Oh, how I needed some people, some friends, to restore the possibility within me that maybe, just maybe, I had gifts to offer. That's what friends do, perhaps. They help us to see what we've forgotten about ourselves or can no longer uncover in ourselves.

Shift to another good friend. He is the kind of person that knows how to make things happen. Professionally he has earned a lot of his credibility by getting things done. He's smart. He's witty. He's thoughtful. He's also quite kind. And willing to reach out. And willing to drop things to make time.

In one of those rather intense despair times for me, I knew that I needed someone to be with me. I just needed some company despite my buy-in to perpetuate my story of figuring it out independently. My despair had me tipping into what was feeling like an irretrievably lost place. Like I was just going to lose it.

I called my friend on a Saturday around 4:30. It took effort for me to make the call. I felt very vulnerable and very pathetic. We exchanged our hellos. And I got to the point. "I really just need to be with someone tonight. I really need a friend." He didn't hesitate. "I'm turning the car around now. I'll be there in 45 minutes." It is a 45-minute drive. That's friendship.

I suppose what still moves me from that experience is that my friend, or anyone, was willing to "come get me." Because I felt so unworthy to be loved. Yup, that's connected to divorce and pains. Yup, that's connected to my version of a not-resolved childhood wound. Yup, that's a deep, deep, inception layer of emotional dislocation. My visiting friend, and others along the way – they helped. In ways that I'm not sure I really deserved. There it is again – shame that is never afraid to drop in unannounced to inform: "You don't deserve love."

We need friends to interrupt such harmful cycles of thought and feeling, that it turns out, are quite common human experience. We need friends to remind us that we belong. And sometimes community. And sometimes family

These poems that follow are about some of the friendship I sought and was fortunate to find. They are about gifts found in waking life friendship, and in association from night-time dreams. They are poems that helped restore my sense of place in my community and human family. They helped restore my sense of being loved, even when living despair.

Today

I think I need a friend,
today.

I can feel myself slipping into more
hermit-like mode,
today,
and for so many of the last days.

It's not more rest that I need,
today.

It's more whole-heartedness
today,
and so many of the coming days.

Real Companionship

I sit on a chair at a small round table.
She is close, in this dream, facing me.
We are laughing.
I hug her head cupping the back of her neck
that brings our foreheads together,
and can sense mutual attraction to intimacy.

Then she is getting her hair ready.
It is long and unkempt, from overnight sleep.
I'm seeing the side of her that few see.

I speak the obvious, about her hair.
"Yes, you have a thing going there."
We both want real companionship.

Old Friend

Old friend,
snuggled with me,
staying close –
thank you
for accepting me.

A Friend's Witnessing

Here are three gifts I see in you,
she said.

You genuinely care.
I see it in how you interact with others.
I see it in your intentional words.
I can feel it.

You balance masculine and feminine.
I see it in your kindness.
I see it in your lightness.
I can feel it.

You are steady.
I see it in your patience.
I see it in your calmness.
I can feel it.

I am grateful
for a friend's witnessing.

When Chemical Meets Alchemical

I have learned
that chemical attraction
is temporary.

However,
it is alchemical attraction
that gives the chemical
its longevity.

I have the feeling
that that matters.

Is This How It Works?

Naked.
Aroused.
Uncomfortable.
Is this how it works?

Continued Laughter

I dreamed of being with her,
playfully,
this friend from so long ago.

She lays on her back.
while I help her stretch her feet and legs.

I love her black pants
and blouse.

I love the feeling of her breasts with first touch,
and her continued laughter.

I love that we know our relationship is
different now.
But that we still laugh together.

Mutual and Unapologetic

The intimacy
I seek
is mutual
and unapologetic.

The intimacy
I seek
is returning
to life.

The intimacy
I seek
has inherent and lasting
friendship.

She Offered Me Her Hand

Tears of ache and loss welled within me,
again.
I wouldn't be able to contain these tears
much longer.

I was tender.
I was raw.
I was aching.

Again.

She offered me her hand to hold,
And squeezed mine
quietly.

That's a friend.

Those Twenty Minutes

Thank you friends,
for coming this way,
for these days together
in joy, play, and thoughtful connection.

Those twenty minutes
sharing stories at days end
made such difference,
and built lasting friendship.

Scented

Their kindness is palpable.
Belonging creates bud.

This folded together,
for these few days,
grows me to flower.

Their kindness
scents me.

I'm glad for that.

Incomprehensible Order

Perhaps the partnering I most seek
is with life itself,
enlivened by the great unknowing
in which there is
incomprehensible order.

Behind That

I think
I'm becoming more interested
in the intimacy and depth
that grows,
sometimes,
ever so naturally,
into the tricky territory
of partnering as human beings.

It's not marriage.
It's not romance.
I want and need what is behind that.

Remarkable Days

I have felt much pleasure
to be in this distant travel with you.

I'm grateful
for your kindness,
for your thoughtfulness,
for your wit,
and for your tumbling forward with yes.

I don't know
what will remain with me
as time repacks this moment.
These have been remarkable days,
opening to the heart.

That's a Friend

"I'd welcome you to lean as far as you want
into that incapacitation you so fear.

I will catch you.
I will blow your nose for you,
feed you food,
and wipe your ass for you.

If you aren't put back together by Wednesday,
I'll take you home with me,
set you up in my room,
place my things around you,
and keep you there."

That's a friend.

So Much Better

"Welcome belonging,"
he encouraged me,
"through who you are."

"It works so much better
than reaching for that
which you wholly aren't."

Friends

Friends
help us
to clear
distortions,
and to reset
boundaries,
in a way
that align us
with life
again.

INTIMACY AND FRIENDSHIPS
Reflection by Ross Billings:

KNOWING AND BEING KNOWN reveals a strength of heart. Imagine Tenneson, tuning his guitar with intimacy, creating the music of friendship. Discovering for men, however brief, an antidote to misery.

CHAPTER 5

FROM THE BOY,
TO THE BOY

TEN YEARS AGO a friend nudged me into giving more attention to my night-time dreams. To write them. To catch them. Up to that point in my life, I would have honestly said that I didn't really dream. Or, that I didn't dream that often. Or, that I didn't remember my dreams. But I know enough now of the psyche's subconscious training facility, and of the physicality of REM sleep, to understand that the dreams are there – just often beyond the threshold or habit of recall.

Ten years ago, when I started journaling my dreams, I wanted to welcome sense-making that was beyond rational and linear brain. I followed my intuition to commit to a habit of writing the dreams – it proved true that as I wrote them, both more dreams came, and, I could remember more of them. Snippets. Images. Sometimes full stories. I was learning immensely from picking symbols from the dreams, then free-associating meanings of the symbols and then following the intuitive soup of it all to recognize the main theme and a few invitations about how to bring the relevance of those night dreams to waking life. It wasn't calcified prescriptions that I sought ("this symbol always means this, and you should do this…") – that kind of stuff just makes me itchy and grumpy. What I did seek was more lenses through which to notice and make sense of an active inner psyche.

I remain really grateful, by the way, for the workshop that I went to in 2013, when the speaker said, "most people feel the night time is to rest and ready ourselves for the day time. Oh, no – the day time is just to prepare us for the night time world of dreaming."

With all of that as context, one particular dream about a boy has been uniquely important to me, one that I had in 2018, in the midst of very thick despair. I would name the general theme of this dream, "retrieving the inner boy." Lost inner child work is rather significant. I've learned that such work and dreams of retrieval are common among many people – it seems a natural need given contemporary western surface patterns of either prematurely ejecting youth to adult life, or the opposite, prolonging and perpetuating blocked passage that renders outwardly appearing adults that are really uninitiated teens in masquerade.

I dreamt that I was in a home that reminded me of the home of a great aunt, my maternal grandfather's sister. It was a home where my grandparents, my two younger cousins, my sister and I would stay overnight on the way to summer holiday and camping. In the dream, I am my current age. I am with a woman also of similar age, who is taking me down into the basement of this home. Instead of stairs, there is a ladder similar to what you would find on the outside of a large tower. It's 40 or 50 feet down.

In the dream, it feels ominous to go down these ladder steps, but I do, ahead of the woman. It's a bit dark, dimly lit at best. One large room, the size of a gymnasium, with a 50-foot ceiling. This basement is unknown to me. There are pillow cushions in this basement, and three couches. In the dream, in this dimly lit basement, I hear faint sounds from behind a sheet-rocked wall. Muffled sounds. But they sound like a human voice. It's not behind a wall that is part of another room. It's walled off. Trapped. It sounds like a boy behind the wall, perhaps ten or twelve years old. I'm looking at the woman I'm with to see if she is hearing the sounds, wondering if I'm imagining them. She seems to be hiding the fact that she is hearing the voice. She goes back up the ladder steps. I'm afraid to stay in the basement. But I decide to do so. I think that there is a boy that is trapped behind the wall. In the dream, I commit to staying with the boy. I wake.

I'm glad for a few people that have helped me to pay attention to the inner boy. Wise family and wise friends. Because I've often resisted it – in waking life I've wanted to leave parts of me behind. The resistance is part of the inner psyche system that protects. As a man, to lean into and inquire more of one's inner boy, is to lean into territory that is so often very unresolved, and very murky. It has vulnerability to it. It has softness in it. It has layers of fear I resisted, despite being a rather willingly vulnerable person. When mental toughness and a desired infallibility is what society has rewarded (rather than awareness and awakeness), the system prevents many of us from the needed retrieval journey.

So, these poems have something to do with that relationship with inner boy, which ironically, has a way of guiding us to being more matured men.

Welcome Them, All of Them

Welcome them,
all of them.

Welcome the skinny and joyful five-year-old
that would climb uninhibitedly on his dad's lap.

Welcome the hurt teen
that cowered, and insisted you be vigilant
and protected.

Welcome the overconfident young man
that so regularly wore mask of arrogance.

Welcome the grown, matured,
and lineaged man,
that has waited with knowing patience,
readied for this time.

Welcome the guide that now grows
life and relationship,
that accepts the trouble needed
that can begin to change everything.

Welcome them, all of them,
with thanks and honor.

Little Boy

Lost from stabilizing mother,
and grown to young adult man
cloaked in bravado –
walk in tandem with me.

Let your scared,
expressionless and numbed face
soften to smile once again.

We can cheer together,
appreciate,
and protect together.

Know that there are many shapes of you
yet to come,
and that underneath all of this,
you are timeless.

Little Boy,
we can walk together.

He Sees Me

I am waiting.

Someone slips in front of me
cheating the line.

He sees this
and makes it right.

Don't Damage This History

Look at these son,
this is the home of your Great,
Great Grandparents.

And this,
of your Great, Great Aunt.

This is the porch
that my Great Grandfather napped on.
I come from people, as do you.

This home is painted white now, emptied,
and readied for sale.

Don't damage this history.
There might be ghosts you aren't ready to face.

He Wept

He wept at her funeral.
"She was my mom.
She was my friend.
I'll miss her."

Hello Little Boy

Hello little boy.
I see you.

Thank you for what you have done.
It is a lot.

You got hurt when you were young.
You got scared and afraid.
You got wounded.

You closed up.
I know that your intent was to protect yourself.

You shut down some of your thinking.
You sought to hide.

I know that you protected me.
And I needed the protection.
We survived together.

Thank you.
I wouldn't be here without you.

Do you want to let go now?
I think you do.

What you've done isn't needed anymore.
Can I just thank you
for your undying attention and vigilance?

We don't need to be a little boy now.
I will always love you.

I will always appreciate
what you did.

And how you were so fierce about it.
Thank you
little boy.

Fathers Day

I celebrate the Fathers I've known.

I celebrate the Fathers In Law, I've known.

I celebrate my Grandfathers,
and those before them.

I celebrate the Grandfathers In Law, I've known.

I celebrate my Uncles that offered Fathering

I celebrate my Friends that are Fathers.

I celebrate the Next Gen that may become
Fathers.

I celebrate Me as Father.
It's been a delight to love and learn in this way.

May this day connect us even more,
in the long arc.

Fathers Day.

Thrice Honored

Before he left,
he made his bed,
knowing I would appreciate it.
He tidied,
and left his pillow signed,
"Dad, love you."

"I'm so glad you are my dad."
She texted,
adding one last note to cap the day.

"Thanks for everything you do.
I'm proud to be your son,
and love all the memories we have
and will make."
He shared.

I felt
honored.

Thirteen Years Ago

Thirteen years ago,
Boy was born.
His skin was very dark.
His eyes were very white.

His birth changed many lives.

I am grateful
in this mystery
that is more
than thirteen years with Boy.

We Three

We sat together,
this influential man and me,
at a restaurant table,
awaiting three others
to join us for lunch.

My 13 year-old boy sat across from us,
and without saying many words,
watched and wondered
what was next.

This connection among we three
was palpable
and nourishing.

That's what honesty
and innocence
and friendship
can do.

I've Had to Learn That

I can be with power.
It is even drawn to me.
I've had to learn that.

Three Things to Remember –
Thank You Mary Oliver

As long as you're dancing,
    you can break the rules.

Sometimes, breaking the rules
    is just extending the rules.

Sometimes,
    there are no rules.

* *A Thousand Mornings*, 2012

A Bit of Tending

I dreamt
that I was standing with them,
an older woman of grandma age,
grayed and wisened,
and of a younger man
who appeared to be in his thirties.

The man was father to a young baby
and seemed to need a bit of help.

I offered to tend his child for a bit,
and reached for the bag of baby supplies.

"Don't you love the spot right here,
where the baby's head fits so well?" I said,
and touched just above my collar bone.

And then, I put my head into that same spot,
just above the collar bone,
of the elder, grayed and wisened woman.

And then,
I woke.

Perhaps,
we all need a bit of tending.

FROM THE BOY,
TO THE BOY
Reflection by Dave Waugh:

THERE IS GREAT TREASURE HIDDEN WITHIN EACH OF US. Sometimes in childhood, we get a glimpse of this treasure, but then, lose sight of it again for many years.

When I was a young boy, growing up through the early 1960s in rural Nova Scotia, I loved to explore the backwoods that led to the shores of the wild Atlantic; especially with my loyal dog, King. That golden time became tarnished the year that I turned eight. My father and Scout Master were drowning in their addiction to alcohol, and the military delivered new orders. I left the glow of my innocence behind with my friends; I left behind my connection to nature and my connection with my beloved canine.

Faithfully held in some deep recesses to be retrieved at a later date, that luminous time remained painfully quarantined within me – even with my growing and consuming habits of overwork and self-medication. These evasive strategies caught up with me in midlife. My marriage failed, I lost my eight-year-old stepson, and my work became vacant and soul-crushing. The only way back to me was to resume my noble maritime adventure of childhood.

I returned to school at the age of 35 and trained as a wilderness guide and, eventually, as a psychotherapist. The dam broke in a remedial English class, where I found myself writing about King, my dog. I became flooded with my repressed grief. The crack in my armour helped me to see how emotionally blocked I had become and how this had impacted all of my relationships.

The journey of discovery and healing is rarely a straight line. Tenneson knows this. Writing down the trouble of life makes it more available to work with and learn from. Tenneson also knows this. A simple passage about an almost-forgotten four-legged friend began a long initiation and apprenticeship in personal healing that led me to retrain in a new career, remarry, reconnect with my stepson and welcome my grandchildren into the world. Only now am I able to help other men – to remember and recover their displaced brilliance, often lost as boys.

CHAPTER 6

SUICIDE

I WAS 14 WHEN MY DAD COMMITTED SUICIDE. It was November 1976. He took pills. His pain was too much for him. He was 34.

I was a boy living in Edmonton, Alberta, with my Mom, only 34 herself, and my older sister, Wendy, aged 15. We were all young.

I learned of my Dad's suicide when I'd come home from playing with one of my childhood friends. It was daytime. I was met at the back door by my Mom and her sister, my Auntie Di. Auntie Di was kind to my friend, telling him he would need to go because "there were some private family issues that needed attention." The women in my family were again tending to what needed tending.

I couldn't see her, but I could hear my Grandma's voice in the living room. That's my Dad's Mom. It was odd that she was there at that time of the day.

My Mom walked me to my bedroom at the end of the hallway in our small Edmonton home. She sat me down on the edge of my bed. It was less than a minute from when I'd entered the back door, but time felt very blurry, happening both fast and slow at the same time.

It was clear to me, in my guts, that something important had happened and that I was about to hear about it. My Mom sat with me on the edge of my bed. She held my 14-year-old hand. Through her own tears, yet with a determinedness that can only come from love, she shared, "I have some sad news to tell you. Your Dad has died."

I wept, not even knowing what my Mom's words really meant. My Dad was dead. Gone. No longer living. A collage of images rushed at me as the shock further enveloped. My Dad that had also been my baseball coach. My Dad that had taken me for scooter rides through fields of ground-feeding seagulls that would scatter in flight as we came near, to my young boy delight. My Dad that held me tight. My Dad that would read the Sunday paper settled to living room chair, dressed only in his underwear. My Dad that made a quarter disappear from his hands and then made it magically appear from my ear. My Dad was dead. Gone. No longer living.

It was that day in November 1976 that changed a lot for me and many people. It was that day that I encountered an edge that would come to be with me, in one form or another, all of my life. I didn't know it then. I came to know it more fully over the coming decades. This loss, to be clear, was not my only edge. And to be clear, I feel that we, all people, have edges we must face. This was a big one for me. Ouch.

As a 14-year-old, I didn't have words nor depth of psychology for it, but later, I would come to realize more about how I felt shame, that I was to blame for my

Dad's death. It's just what kids do in such circumstances. And what I also did then, is that I began internalizing at another layer. I became more reserved. More inward. More wanting to deny the ouch. I'm so lucky to have had good people, good women and men in my family and family's friends – it could have been much worse.

Fast forward thirty-five years, years that included a lot of good living. Love. Family. Vocation. Friendships. Travel. And loss. Background grief. Anxiety. Fulfillment. They all go together. When shock, or trauma, or wound appears, one path is to get reflective about it. Eventually, I did.

Fast forward to an important conversation with a good friend, with whom I've talked about suicide a few times. My Dads and mine. Not ideation.

"Of course there is a part of you that wants to die," he told me. I'd shared my desire to die, the shame that I'd felt with it. The grief. The despair. I'd shared some of the ways that my Dad's suicide had impacted me. I'd shared fears. Fear of loss. Fear of intimacy. Fear of failure. Fear of shame. All of which yoked me to suicide.

It was that day, when my friend said, "Of course there is a part of you that wants to die," that a bunch of my relationship with suicide began to transform.

My friend spoke a wisdom, plain and simple, that I hadn't been able to find.

He helped me to feel the normalness of wanting relief. He helped re-context the desire for departure much more universally. It was becoming clear, insights flooding in, that helped to crack through my habit of thought. I was waking to how these deeply personal and shameful thoughts were much more universal. I was finding path – learning that death is one of the ways that some seek to remove themselves from suffering. Just like my Dad. There are parts of ourselves – emotions, stories, memories – that we naturally want to shed. I was learning to distinguish: shedding and leaving is related to suicide, but not the same thing.

These poems come from my relationship with suicide. My Dad's. My own desire to get out of the pain. Of loss. Of shame. Of fatigue. Of overwhelm. I'm so glad for a friend that invited some normalcy in the shame and the deep wound, to lean in and come to walk with the despair, rather than away from it.

Hmm...

There are times
in this human life
when I want to go away.

Some times
I can't quite find my way back
from dreams
and the other hidden worlds.

Some times
I don't want to find my way back.

Hmm...

Enslaved by Story

In the story that enslaves me,
I am broken.
The facade that is me
can no longer sustain anything.
I am spiralling out of control,
shamed to realize how insignificant I am
and how futureless my future is.

I rock myself to sleep
wishing for deliverance.
I dream of being lost.
I wake in the night
only to find that I can't escape.
Another tear falls down my cheek
as I become aware that I must face another day.

I feel myself as a wasteland.

Aloneness Scares Me Most

The aloneness scares me most.
It touches a deep and old wound.

A voice whispers.

"Give them back their separation."
"Give him back his death."

Last Day?

I am aware of my fear
that has me grasping and pretending,
"What if this were my last day to live in this life?"

Yes, it's suicidal.
Of course a part of me wants to die.

I feel a relief
in the thought
that this might be it.

I also feel shame.

I am finding it
harder and harder
to feel vitality.

With yet another
brush of despair,
and shame,
I try again.

I look to name what is good in this moment,
of this beginning
of this day,
just as people have told me I should.
The large shower in the room in which I stay.
The music I play to quiet my fears.
The shirt I'm wearing, a recent gift
from my daughter and son in-law.
The people I'll meet today.

One more morning
of one more day –
it's all I can see.

The Monastery I Crave

Perhaps I am living
in the monastery
that I crave.

It is not ancient stone walls.
It is my sheet-rocked home.

My monastery
is not a community of monks
deprived of material goods.

I have TV.
I have food.
I have phone.
I have computer.

But let's be clear.
I now live alone.

And I suppose,
that a significant part of me
wants,
or needs,
to live alone.

I'm getting the solo,
and much-feared,
experience
that I've avoided.

Perhaps, beyond the immediate hurt,
I'm right on track.

Crazy in It

This life,
it seems to me,
remains a confusing mystery.

I've been taught to fit in,
to adhere to systems of belief and behavior.
That is where so much of my belonging
has occurred.

The team.
The family.
The community.
The church.

I've also been taught to challenge the edges.
To stay true to myself.
To seek another way and to explore it fully.

In the best of moments,
I've experienced belonging
in the company of those willing
to explore the edges.

We seem to share a belief
that "all is not what it seems."

However, to insist on new edges
with people that don't seek the edge
– well, this is somewhat alienating
and disappointing.
Not the best match for me.

I don't know how much longer
I can live in that world.

It feels crazy.
I feel crazy in it.

This Is Real

I didn't sleep well,
again,
last night.

That's what despair does.
It keeps us up in the night,
reprieved from the next day.

It takes effort,
living in this depression,
to not just give up
and lie in bed all day.

After these awake nights
in which
I hope they go slow
so that morning doesn't come too soon
and another day
in which
I pretend to be
getting along just fine.

I want to shake it.
But I don't.
Or can't.

This is real.

Come Lineage

Come lineage,
please,
I beg you.
Make it true
that time
is not
linear.

Dad.
Uncles.
Grandparents.

I need you,
now,
in this place
of utter
loneliness.

The Wobble

This is the wobble of despair
that comes in morning with added vigor,
that has me crying out for help
from my bed
or the corner floor
in which I've collapsed.

It's OK to need help,
I hope.

It's OK to be honest and unashamed about it,
I hope.

Too Much

I am not OK.
I don't want to live.
It's just too much.

Might Not Make It Out

I once travelled
with old and reliable friends,
and a few younger people too,
in need of favor.

We drove through deep, snow-filled woods,
following a track laid by those before us,
edging our way along,
careful to keep up.

Inevitably,
however,
we found ourselves
in our own isolated stuckness.

It's then,
though we could still see
lights ahead
of those before us,
that we learned that this is the kind of stuck
that we might not make it out of.

The Big Gamble

The big gamble, I feel, in this life, is that
it is worth it to interrupt pattern.
It is worth it to challenge the default story.
It is worth it to awake from numbing.
It is worth it to attempt truth that
I can't fully articulate.

The big gamble, I feel, in this life, is that
interrupting patterns makes a difference.
Saying no to default commercialism.
That systemic and societal overload
isn't personal.
That whole-heartedness is in fact
antidote to exhaustion.

The big gamble, is that it really matters.
Because sometimes I wonder if the blue pill
would just be easier.

Relieve

I wonder if death is just a more attractive offer.
To relieve myself of the pain of this life.
To relieve myself of the pain of the choices
that I've made in this life.

I wonder if I'm now wandering
beyond the point of sanity
and beyond the point of return.

Panic Attack

I'm living
a panic attack
of fear
at the losses
that feel
just too much
to bear.

Utterly Spent

I've never felt so fucked up in my entire life.

That means insecure.
That means doubtful.
That means lost.
That means unmoored.
That means dreading the commitments
I ought to fulfill.

In family.
In marriage.
In career.
In friendship.

It all comes together
in these moments of
utterly spent.

Low Confidence

What I don't like in these days,
is that my confidence is low
and I'm not trusting my instinct.

Trying So Hard

Often
I feel
that I can't go on.

The immensity
of trying
to prove
myself
is exhausting
and very dissatisfying.

Why
must
I try
so hard?

What
in me
has convinced myself
that I must
try so hard?

Stay Interested

What does it take to be OK with self?
I do not know the answer to this.

I do know that it helps
to stay interested 'till the end.

SUICIDE

Reflection by Tom Inglis:

THIS WORK STANDS ON ITS OWN and will have meaning and create an opportunity for reflection in those who read it. Tenneson's poetry, like music, has a way of striking a chord, a resonance within us that we can't explain, a chemical reaction that just happens when the elements are in close proximity. The mind can play tricks and make the familiar "better than it really is" and perhaps the work strikes me that way as it definitely has another layer of meaning in knowing the poet, the friend, the father, and the man. If you haven't had the pleasure of meeting, knowing and loving Tenneson, in this work he shows up in honesty and gives you a chance through these poems to do so. Writing in the first person, there is no doubt whose thoughts, feelings, experiences these are. Perhaps it is that radical transparency on these taboo topics, of depression, anxiety and suicide that hits the mark. Like a tethered arrow to the heart, I feel these poems, tugging on old scars. They also tug on the fear of not knowing where our friends, loved ones and even ourselves are at. Where in the inner landscape of the soul do we find ourselves? Will we be OK?

This section on the theme of suicide shines a light on the darkest thoughts of the human psyche. By taking a picture with words of those thoughts, those dark days, the poet draws a map of the landscape of depression.

From that place of despair, he asks the unspeakable questions: How can I go on? Why should I go on? Perhaps this is the day from which I do not go on? Within the darkest of the dark days, the glimmer of hope: "Perhaps beyond this immediate hurt I am right on track;" "Perhaps everything is not as it seems." A poetic journey around the idea that we are not our thoughts, we are not our depression and we are not our perspectives, marks a path through the valley of self-abandonment. The shame and heaviness of these poems remind us to make no mistake, "This is real."

In perhaps one of the most famous poems by the poet Dylan Thomas, "Do not go gentle into that good night," we are reminded of our mortality, that we all face death, darkness and yet we can choose how we face that "Dying of the light...";

CHAPTER 7

SIMPLE

A FRIEND REMINDS ME of a quote from Oliver Wendell Holmes, a former American judge and writer. It's a quote that I often use in my facilitation work with groups, teams and communities when I'm trying to invite people to deeper layers of learning and insight. It matters, for many of us, to find the simple, but to also pay attention to where that simplicity comes from. Says Holmes, "I would not give a fig for the simplicity on this side of complexity, but I would give my life for the simplicity on the other side of complexity."

Such a statement guides me, and many of us, to navigate and explore the roots of our pains. Or, to wander and wonder into what is behind our persistent yearnings. Or, to follow and befriend longings that help us find our way in the woods. Simplicity on the other side of complexity encourages each of us to go more fully toward life's initiating moments, beckoning us to not be satisfied with the superficial.

I continue to learn that finding essence and simplicity is less like shopping for an item in a grocery store, available upon demand. It's more like awaiting a flowering spring bulb to rise from the ground, which comes only with its own natural timing. I continue to learn that finding essence and simplicity grounds me with a gift of guiding principles, and of being clear at a gut layer amidst complex things.

For example, when I was in divorce, and the deep grief and shame that came with it, I needed to claim a simple headline that was true, yet brief. I needed a narrative arc that honored some of the hopes, dreams, and loss. I needed to find it for myself, and, for sharing with others. "We were very important people in each other's' lives – until we weren't." Of course, that's not all of it. But there is a kindness in the simplicity of "just enough."

When it comes to simplicity, I'm aware that simplicity can be, well, oversimplified (the stuff on this side of complexity). A certain nuance of simplicity can trick us into avoidance from a needed, and more complicated awareness. Simplicity can also be a cop-out to avoid the heavy lifting of difficult personal exploration. These are all nuances that we each must face and learn.

There is some found simplicity, thankfully, in these poems. I've written most of them from the still fresh enough slumber of night rest, before the rational and logical brain could take over. I've written, sometimes in very brief phrases, welcoming and befriending the kind of essence that Holmes references. I haven't tried to offer every bit of context. They aren't meant to have misdirection, but they are meant to extend a bit of permission to dwell in the simple.

In The Simple

I love the way
that horses graze in a nearby field.

Sometimes the young ones run
in short spurts.

I love the way
that birds sing in morning sky.

Sometimes a chirp,
sometimes a whistle.

I love the way
that horses and birds remind me
to live
in the simple.

This Might Be Some of My Best Thinking Ever

Don't think too much.

Only

Be simple.
Be clear.

Do only
what you would feel excited
about doing.

Just for a little.

Stay in Breath

"Stay in breath,"
she reminds me.

Most people,
it turns out,
have forgotten to breathe.

Yesterday
I gave myself permission
to not think.

Really,
I gave myself permission
to feel.
And to not fear.

These are the breaths
that make a difference.

Not My Covenant, Again

"Security," come excite me again.
"Power," come comfort me again.

Ah, you are only dreams, again.

Your price of my required abandonment of self,
and tarnished authenticity,
so as to fit in,
aren't what I want.

I don't want to live that lie, again.
That is not my covenant, again.

I Don't Like

I don't like your imposition
of your insecurity

because

I don't like the confrontation it creates in me
with my insecurity.

No Words

I'm ready for the space of no words.
I'm ready for the space of nothing.

So as to welcome arising.
Or maybe, just emptying.

A Tea Day

It's definitely a tea day.

By that I mean
a day for detox.

To recover from
this re-opened wound,

to find ground from
this re-opened trauma

and to steady my nerves from
all the shaking and rattling.

Too much noise
means I need some silence

and tea.

I Have Three Needs

I have three needs.

Vibrant.
Alive.
Awake.

Wanting to feel vibrant.
Wanting to feel alive.
Wanting to feel awake.

Not, dimmed.
Not, protecting and conserving.
Not, sleepy in soul.

As If We Matter

I don't know the woman that runs near me,
in this community event.
But she is kind, and feels like family.
She stops to help a man, admirably,
that had fallen behind her,
who then showed her no interest or gratitude.

I continue with this woman I don't know,
running slightly ahead of her, encouraging her.
I wish that she would pass me.
For her good.

There is no clear finish in this race.
It doesn't even matter that it is a race.
It just matters to treat self, and other
as if we matter.

Adapt

In first moment,
I'm very good,
clear.

Then,
I'm impeded,
with trouble that distracts.

But then,
adapting,
I do what needs to be done.

Betraying Self

I seek to belong,
but have learned,
that the price of abandoning self,
of betraying self,
for belonging,
is not at all sustainable.

Think Less

Think less.
Feel more.

Plan less.
Presence more.

Doubt less.
Trust more.

Release.
Give to.

Tumble forward.
Surrender.

Fried Onions and Red Peppers

He brought me a plate of fried onions
and red peppers.
It was a kind gesture.
Simple.

It's good to be cared for.

Great Pain

I caused great pain.
This is true.

It's just not all that happened.

Before Me

What is before me,
holds enough,
to make sense,
of it all.

What if that were true?

What if,
in the "anything" before me,
is the "everything"
that welcomes being understood.

There is a simple
that perhaps stops us
from the incessant search
for too much.

Own

Can
I
own
the
contradictions
in
me?

Blessing

Today, I'll take the blessing
from the unseen,
thank you.

No, I'm not all well.
I just need and want the blessing,
whatever that is.

Fuck Off

Fuck off.
I've wallowed enough to know wallow's full
taste.

Fuck off.
I've capitulated and surrendered,
prostrated abundantly.

Fuck off.
I've asked questions upon questions.
I've explored and, it's a given that,
I will continue to do so.

Fuck off.
I'm clear.

Fuck off.
I've learned, I'm ready.

Fuck off.
I need my fire too.

Acquired in Intimacy

I have interest in intimacy.
In connection.
In companionship.
These are all very important to me.

I also have wound
and trauma
acquired in intimacy.

People who love each other
sometimes hurt each other.

Fair

Is it fair?
I'm not sure.

I Continue to Learn

I continue to learn
that it is important to seek not just patterns,
but also,
what is below them.

I continue to learn
that it is important to live not just with safety,
but also,
with willingness to go to the edge.

Only Momentary

This place
is only a stopping ground,
attractive for its illusion
of permanence
and stability.

This place
is most lasting
in the awareness
that it is
only momentary.

When Strangers Take Us In

There are times in our lives
  when strangers take us in.

They pilot us to temporary landing.
They offer us a shared meal
  from what they have.
They welcome us to their friends,
  and to their kin.

They give us home
  until we can sort ourselves out,
  until we can remember
  enough of who we are.

I'm glad for that.

SIMPLE

Reflection by Robert Gareau:

T HERE ARE GOOD REASONS why we often seek
to simplify things in our lives. When we enter
periods of darkness and encounter the many troubles
that accompany them, it is comforting to break things
down into smaller, more manageable pieces. It is why
we are often looking for that off switch or mute button,
or at least the volume down control. The expression
"less is more" comes to mind and it is often the little
acts of kindness and small gestures that can have large
impacts.

In this Chapter, Tenneson uses his words in a most
efficient manner to create short, concise poems that
convey his feelings in a powerful, essential way. I
admire his courage to face his despair and his
willingness to share his gifts with us. These compact
verses shine with purity of thought and leave me with
feelings of being transported to a world that has been
cleared of all the clutter and distractions that I usually
encounter.

The poems in this Chapter are authentic, direct,
    clear,
        honest,
            pure,
                elemental,
                    and simple.
Powerful!

CHAPTER 8

BIRTH AND NEW LIFE

"OKNESS", THE GERMINATION OF NEW LIFE, of psyche, and of fruitful surrender, didn't arrive on a set date for me. It wasn't a plan that I'd written down, nor a goal that I'd set, nor a particular orchestrated moment on which I'd imagined arising from despair. It was not that, despite my clear begging for immediacy of relief so many times.

I remember an August morning, 2019, sitting on my balcony. It was early. It was quiet. Skies were a bit cloudy. As the sun rose over the Wasatch Mountains east of me, and its light and warmth began to wake the day, there was a moment of waking for me, more palpably, to "I'm going to be OK." It's the morning that I wrote the poem, "I'm OK," included near the end of this chapter.

This waking may not sound like much, this "I'm OK." But beneath those words lived a quiet inner-resolvedness and feeling of "a-ha," or of "new vision," or of "earned passage," as if I'd worked hard enough at the puzzle of despair and now had the right to integrate that to "OKness." It was as if, perhaps, I'd done enough penance, enough beating myself, enough shaming, enough persistence with despair – to be blessed to move through. My palpable "OKness" felt like that moment when the first yellow or orange leaf of autumn, releases its hold to tree, and signals the shift of season. I felt that kind of change. That kind of quiet knowing. That kind of initiatory passage, where enough of a wound had been filled with gold and I could see again in the dark woods.

Two months later, in the autumn of 2019, I also had another significant newly-dawned awareness, to realize that it had been months since I'd woken in the night with "please, please, please God – help me make it through this day." I was a bit surprised to realize this, the way that sometimes time just takes over, healing us with its blurred passing. Blurred like when you can't remember the last time you watched a movie – seems like it was a month ago, but really, was a year ago. Time had passed. Something had passed more in me. I wasn't begging.

To be clear, I don't feel completely removed from despair. Nor do I feel that is the point. Those 20oz cans of ache, and challenge, and panic, and loss, and despair in my kitchen cupboard remain where they are – I just don't feel obligated to them in the same way. They don't fall to the counter each time I open the cupboard, demanding my cleanup. I have more choice. I just formed – or was blessed with, or enough time passed for, or had some dumb luck granting – a different relationship with the pleading and begging. It moved on. Or me. Or both.

Or, maybe the leaf simply fell, as it was inevitably bound to do.

These poems, point to some of that birth, to the new that comes not from avoiding and leaning further away, but rather, from facing the seasons, and staying with the path in the dark woods, leaning in further to self and to community – from which new life and path can arise.

When The Veil Is Thin

Perhaps
there is a veil of awareness
that is thin
during the night.

At 2:50,
I don't
particularly want
to lay awake
fretting
over the rest
I'm not getting.

But,
perhaps,
in the night,
there is deep connection
with spirit.

When the veil is thin,
I learn.

I've Earned Trouble

The heat is too much.
I flake.
I peel.

Yet, thankfully,
I'm intact.

I'm relieved.
I wake.

Old life, go.
I departed.
I've earned new trouble.
Undeniably, in new life.

Living Alone

He was gentle in his nudge.
I think he saw the stuck point in me.
I think he saw that the change I needed
was on the inner,
not the outer.

There is no need to punish yourself.
There is much that is delicious
in your isolation
and in the freedom
of your circumstance.

You should think
about living alone.

Medicine

Wander.
It is some of the best medicine
I know.

Change.
Wash off the caked and dried mud
that has covered you.

Welcome.
The bumblebee at dusk,
hovering in echinacea flowers.

Your tears welling,
as you watch the bee backlit by sunset,
are medicine.

I Want To Be With Life

Flow with life itself.

When I think of this,
something feels alive in me.

I don't want to mindlessly be
in the story of this era
and its illusions.

I want to be with life.

Less noise.
More grounding.

Less rush.
More presence with.

Heart Whole

Where I find life
is in tiny bits of kindness,
sometimes, just me giving to me.

In remembering
that there is finite earth time,
and space,
in a day.

In reclaiming awareness
that there need not be time
to blame me
for what is systemic and societal overload.

Where I find life
is in tiny bits of
my heart whole.

Redemption

Be with life.

Redemption in a sentence of three words.

Perhaps Defiantly

The sky feels forever gray,
as far as I can see.

Soft gray.
Not steel gray.

It's not fog.
It's thicker, like cloud.

Leafless trees,
some of them forty feet tall,
stand resistantly,
perhaps defiantly, in waiting for spring.

Roofs of houses
hold off layers of snow,
while steam from heat vents
rises from inner warmth.

Flakes of snow
blow sporadically past my window
while I sit inside
comforted by slippers and a warm sweater.

It's winter.
I watch.

The trees will have their time.
Me too.

I hope,
in Spring.

I Suppose

I suppose I want to fall in love.
I suppose I want to feel loved.
It might be her, I suppose.
Or it might be another person.

I suppose my starting point
is to fall in love with me.

Transformed

I thought this flowing water
was simple backyard stream.
Yet,
it became mighty river.

I thought this crevice was temporary ditch
from last night's storm.
Yet,
it became vast canyon.

There is wonder
in being transformed.

I Wish, I Wish

I wish, I wish
with all my might
for ease
and connection in life.

I wish, I wish
with all my might
for courage
to confront
that which distracts
or manipulates
with well-disguised malice.

I wish, I wish
with all my life
to feel oneness,
home,
love of self,
love of other,
love from self,
love from other.

I wish, I wish
with all my life
for ease,
for belonging,
for release of worry.

Told Things

I want to remember these two things.

He tells me,
"I love the way that spirit swirls in you."

She tells me,
"Your grounding and your authenticity
are really energizing."

It's good,
sometimes,
to be told things.

Inexorably Guided

Perhaps this stage of life,
and my offering,
is to further lean in to the mystic experience.

To see what I see,
what others might not be able to see.
Perhaps, life has been inexorably guiding me.

Dwelling

There are many rooms
in this dwelling.

There is sun here.
There is a balcony
with lots of plants and flowers,
and even a few empty pots.

There is space here
unlocked for my dwelling.

Everybody Loves You

"Everybody loves you,"
she said?

"Really?"
I asked,
liking the sound of it,
but kind of afraid to disconfirm it.

"Yes,"
she said, again.
"Oh, thank you,"
I said softly.

Letting Go

Sometimes
it is letting go
that makes the most
difference.

Everythingness
can be found
at the bottom of
nothingness.

What If, What If?

What if, what if,
this life could be lived
as connection to the infinite?

What if, what if,
the infinite were found
in but a thimble of experience?

What if, what if,
those thimbles of experience
were available anywhere?

What if, what if,
anywhere changed everywhere?

Life is but a dream,
calling for our waking
to the infinite of the every day.

Spacious Skies

This place reminds me of home.
The spacious skies.
The scent.

I seek the scent of home within me.
And spacious skies.

Remember How to Go Quietly

Maybe the world is just noisy,
a cacophony of stimulation overload.

Maybe it is essential
to remember how to go quietly.

Unknown Wander of Time

I am lost.
I am not found.
I am blind.
I do not see.

I need space.
Emptiness.
I don't want filler.
It's too much.
I want to believe that, perhaps,
for an unknown wander of time,
this lost and not found,
this blind and not seeing,

is perfect.

I Want to Bend Time

Days are ticking by, relentlessly,
as if quickened,
and bending toward more and more
fast passings.

It is June.
Where did May go?
And April?
And the first half of the year?

In my mind, it could well be
the first month of the year.
Yet the calendar proclaims to me
the approach of half-way.

I want to bend time.
Perhaps, to slow it down.
Perhaps, just because I can,
and that is what time has been teaching me.

I don't want more days of
living outside of myself.
I don't want more days of
scrambling for a score, or validation.

I want more days of arriving.
To this place, and this time, with welcome.

Familiar

After long journey,
arrived at land ever distant,
it is being met by friends
that makes this return
familiar.

Moments

I want to learn more to relax into the moment
in front of me.
To give myself to it, in joy and openness.
Without fear.
Without worry.
Just totally welcoming.

It's not all moments that I will welcome this way.
There is, after all, pain and suffering.
Yet, more often,
I'm simply living a delightful, unfolding life.
Why not welcome it, and be with it?

I long to be able
to give myself to the moment
that doesn't measure moments,
but flows, trustingly and compellingly,
with the whole of it.

Far From Ordinary

I think that I'm finding a commitment within me.
It's been growing for many years.
Perhaps all of my life.
Perhaps even, lifetimes before that.
This life of mine is far from ordinary,
and thus, it is ripe for a generational change.

I think that I'm finding a commitment within me
to live beyond fear,
beyond protection,
beyond worry,
and to give myself to the source
that is life living me.

I like this feeling.

What I Heard

Rest in what is.
You are loved, just as you are.
You are enough.
You are wildly exciting
in your heart, belly, mind, and spirit.
Let go of all the chatter.
Rest in what is.

Boasting and Sparing

Men often boast
of professional
and financial success.

It appears casual,
but it's really old,
just without literal spears and swords.

Men often spar
in an arena
meant to mask
personal insecurity.

But,
to be fair,
what men often really want
is a belonging
and worth
that lives
beyond
boasting and sparing.

Sealed Over Places

In this period of change,
silly little things
are indicative of important bigger things.

I don't want the first thing of my morning
to be opening my computer.
Rather, I want to catch my dreams
in hand-written color.

I don't want to sit in my regular chair.
I want to see my kitchen, and me,
from another perspective.

I don't want to remain closed to feeling.
Rather, I want to open,
even the sealed over places.

I'm OK

The decks are cleared.
A new day has come.

May it now be
that I move freely
and with freshness
in clear and divine flow
from headwaters abundantly within,
and without,
and among.

I am Ok.

This Much I Know

Follow the spark of yes,
to be in learning,
and to be in community.

Trust that there is guidance,
even providence,
to take me and us,
swinging beyond the edge of the known.

I am mostly convinced
that there is
self
organizing
naturally.

We all have inner longing;
and we all need community to grow courage,

This much I know.

BIRTH AND NEW LIFE
Reflection by John Hoover:

POETRY IS METAPHOR; it leaves space for interpretation, ambiguity, nuance and creative spirit. Poetry is also looking where we don't want to look. Our new learning comes from that confrontation. We've already looked where we want to look. We must die to the known to be born from the unknown.

It is important to think about the parts of ourselves that want to die, while not getting overly identified with them. Like confronting a drowning person, being pulled under is not very useful. Something, and not everything, but certainly some part, must die – even if it's just the weight of panic and despair – in order to claim, and be claimed by, the new life.

Tenneson is a good model of this kind of "survival swimming" in the depths.

EPITAPH

With Gratitude

Gratitude to you, all of us,
who stay with these most difficult
yet important paths of learning,
into the dark woods.

Gratitude to you, all of us,
in these arcs of healing,
that begin with honesty
and friendship.

Gratitude to you, all of us,
who offer our gifts
found in courage,
and trust of a cadence.

AFTERWORD

HOLY WHOLENESS
R o b i   G a r e a u

T ENNESON IS ONE OF THE MOST "WHOLE"
PEOPLE THAT I KNOW. I feel this in a noticeably
organic way whenever I'm in his presence, regardless
of setting or context. It can be difficult to describe, yet it
feels undeniably precious to me in the vacuum of not
really knowing exactly what it is. I suppose there is a
particular blend of traits in the wholeness that he
exudes, one that can feel even holy to me at times.

Those of us fortunate enough to have worked with
him would certainly describe him as smart, thoughtful,
witty, soulful and gracious. As both a facilitator and
friend, he is skilled in dialogue. The kind of dialogue
that leaves a person feeling truly seen. He approaches
conversation with adventurous care and genuine
curiosity – a kind of playful nod to the sacred
exploration of what it means to be human together.

The collection of poems contained in this body of
work is a worthy tribute to this spirit of wholeness. In
the context of doing the work that heals us, curiosity
coupled with courage will make so much more of the
inner landscape visible. Tenneson's honest disclosures,
confessions, ramblings, musings, and raw unfiltered

emotions are offered to us as a guided traverse into the wholeness of the human soul and psyche. Any worthy journey of this kind will eventually enter a darker territory. A territory for which the maps we carry will often feel sketchy. Deep in that darkness, if we dare to enter willingly, lies the golden thread that leads us back to our whole selves.

May this be so for many of us. May we enter willingly.

ABOUT THE AUTHOR

T e n n e s o n   W o o l f

TENNESON WOOLF is a writer, teacher, facilitator, and coach through his company, Tenneson Woolf Consulting. He is often traveling in the wide world, working as a facilitator and workshop leader in the realms of leadership and community engagement, committed to improving the quality of collaboration and imagination needed in groups, teams, and organizations – to help be in times such as these with consciousness, kindness, and learning. Although originally from Edmonton, Alberta, Tenneson now calls Lindon, Utah home – a small town at the foot of the Wasatch Mountains, where urban meets rural – but the call of his Canadian birthplace keep tugging at his roots. Tenneson holds a Masters Degree in Organizational Behaviour and a Bachelors Degree in Psychology. Tenneson has three children, an old camper trailer that once belonged to his maternal grandparents, and a relatively new kayak. A Cadence of Despair is Tenneson's first published book of poetry. You can find Tenneson at www.tennesonwoolf.com, and more about this book at www.centrespoke.com.

INDEX OF POEMS

Made in the USA
Monee, IL
01 May 2020

29330796R00148